WARM BLOODED TREE

Poems by

NINA BELÉN ROBINS

Thompson & Columbus, Inc., Publishers
New York

ISBN: 978-0-9832275-8-8

Cover and Book Design
Mark Wedemeyer / Carbon13 Design Bureau

www.thompsonandcolumbus.com

FOR DION

ALSO BY NINA BELÉN ROBINS

Supermarket Diaries

A Bed With My Name On It

T. Gondii

"The best thing for being sad," replied Merlin, beginning to puff and blow, "is to learn something. That's the only thing that never fails. You may grow old and trembling in your anatomies, you may lie awake at night listening to the disorder of your veins, you may miss your only love, you may see the world about you devastated by evil lunatics, or know your honour trampled in the sewers of baser minds. There is only one thing for it then — to learn. Learn why the world wags and what wags it. That is the only thing which the mind can never exhaust, never alienate, never be tortured by, never fear or distrust, and never dream of regretting. Learning is the only thing for you. Look what a lot of things there are to learn."

T.H. White, author of *A Once and Future King*

CONTENTS

PROLOGUE

WARM BLOODED TREE   *3*

PART ONE: LOVE OR LACK THEREOF

SMOLDER   *6*

BOY IN THE BATHROOM   *8*

QUIET CAR   *10*

DOLLAR STORE   *11*

INFOMERCIAL   *12*

THE DINER   *14*

VALENTINE'S DAY   *16*

VACANCY   *18*

BLUES CLUES   *19*

BARS   *21*

MY LIBIDO, MY CHOICES   *22*

CHURCH STEPS   *24*

CREDIT CARDS AND CELL PHONES   *26*

HOTEL   *27*

THE STAR OF THE SHOW   *28*

PART TWO: THE SAVING OF THINGS

WIZARD   30

MERRY CHRISTMAS   31

MALL WALKERS   32

THROUGH THE GAP   33

PANCAKES AND ORANGE JUICE   35

BOW   36

LEARNING TO SAY NO   38

TIMID MAN   40

EPILOGUE

HOW TO LOVE SOMEONE WHO HAS NEVER BEEN
LOVED (OR HOW TO LEARN TO LOVE AGAIN)   44

WARM
BLOODED
TREE

PROLOGUE

WARM BLOODED TREE

Cleopatra is a cold blooded snake.
I always knew reptiles were cold blooded, always cold,
dependent on external heat sources to stay alive.
We keep Cleopatra warm in her tank with heat lights,
spraying her down daily so her skin doesn't dry.
Without us she wouldn't survive the cold room where she lives.

Cleopatra is a ball python.
I tell people I let her wrap herself around me, and they shudder.
Tell me to be careful,
never trust that she won't bite.

I am not in danger.
She wraps around my outstretched arms in comfort.
To her I am nothing more than a warm tree,
my heart pumping warmth her skin craves,
my pulse keeping her body temperature
as comfortable as the light she lives under the rest of the day.
She feeds off my heat and rests peacefully in my arms.
She trusts me, my body a safe place for her to rest.

Every time my heart breaks
my blood turns cold, heart hardens.
I pile extra blankets on my bed,
rely on thermostats and sweat pants;
the safety of my room enough heat to keep me warm.
I have sworn off love countless times,
forgetting the comfort of a body next to mine.

What are we but cold blooded creatures,
dependent on light and heat to live,
needing love and outstretched arms to wrap around our bodies.
We can warm ourselves with heat lamps and radiators,
but nothing compares to the safety of a warm blooded tree.

PART ONE:

Love or Lack Thereof

SMOLDER

Bobby Flay has the perfect
BBQ sauce for your first date.
There's a side of salmon in the smoker,
the perfect hamburger.

I want to take a bath in the sauce,
he gushes.
Your new partner
will love you forever
when you cook her this.
Crab and Angus meat,
thirty-dollar cooking wine,
three-course protein.
How could this not be a perfect
start to love?

Last week he cancelled
his estranged wife's credit card.
She signed the prenup,
she can't back down.
The articles on Google
exclaim the hate,
how he sprinted
to divorce papers:
the war.

This morning on TV
he shows you how to woo
someone with crab BBQ.

Bring a bottle of Pinot Noir
he tells you.
You'll melt together.

Love promotion
oozing through the cheese
and juices.

He eats
dinner alone in front of a fake tree,
a camera crew,
a smoldering grill
slowly dying in the background.

BOY IN THE BATHROOM

The day the boy took me to the bathroom,
my hair wasn't brushed like usual.

I checked my breath, it was OK,
we went into the boys' dorm,
the one above the cafeteria.

This was going to be my first kiss in a year,
we didn't know each other's names.

I sat on the windowsill, puckered up.
He fell to the floor, kissed my feet instead.

I didn't have time to apologize
for the athlete's foot, nylons,

he stayed there five minutes
just necking with my ankle

until staff knocked on the door
and he yelled out,

I'm taking a shit!
It's fine, I'll be down to lunch in a minute!

using the excuse of watching
staff's feet under the door to keep kissing mine,

my neck lonely for this attention
just glancing out the window
at the snow outside.

We never spoke again after that.
My friends would yell out, *foot fetish!*
when he came around, but that's all.

I think his name was John.
I think I wouldn't have minded if he kissed me.
My feet weren't the ones who were lonely.

Even the boy I gave the bathroom to
only took what he wanted.

QUIET CAR

I'm in the quiet car,
commuters tired and pre-coffee,
haven't finished sleeping,

so when the retching
began it was audible.
At first no one getting up to change cars,

eyes zooming in on screens,
books, Kindles,
as the projectile vomiting echoed.

Finally two people left, some stared
at the occupied light,
ten minutes passed, twenty,

not knowing if death was in the car,
some incurable disease.
Finally a woman the color

of the walls emerged,
stumbling into the next car.

Then silence. Heartbeats.
Back to the screens.

A woman purging her life into a train toilet
forgotten in the announcement for
Grand Central.

DOLLAR STORE

They sell pregnancy tests
at the dollar store, on the wall
by the nail clippers, ChapSticks,
just before you get to the register.

They cost a buck-fifty,
99.9% effective.
The lady behind the counter
says they're the highest selling item.

More than the kitchen utensils
in the last aisle,
the Mylar balloons decorating
the whole left side of the store,
the discounted soaps,
plastic cups and glasses.

I wonder who lines up to buy them.
Who goes in, perhaps looking
at the fake toothpaste,
expired soup, last year's Halloween candy.

If they buy a bag of potato chips
for a quarter, some one-dollar makeup.

Like this is any other
stop in the dollar store.
No big deal, really.

Just a Milky Way,
a pregnancy test.
Just a casual
let-me-know what's on its way.

INFOMERCIAL

In the night before dawn,
your eyes glazed at half-mast,
you watch TV
and learn all the problems of the world
can be solved in four payments of $19.95.

On Monday it's weight loss!
Lose ten pounds and sixteen inches!
That's what John did!
John is stressed, like you!
A single parent, like you!
Has bills, like you!
A mortgage, like you!
Your pants feel tight,
maybe in twenty-five minutes a day
you too can lose those inches.

Tuesday is juicer day!
Vitamins!
Glowing skin!
Shiny hair!
You feel your dry skin,
thinning hair.
If you call in ten minutes
you'll get a free towel!
You think of your towels,
so ordinary,
wonder if you are ordinary too.

Wednesday is for makeup!
Makeover day!
Hide your wrinkles!
Sunspots!

Blemishes!
The actress from
ten years ago
with flawless skin
promising your transformation.
Under the light in the bathroom
you have bags, and wrinkles,
wonder what it is to be beautiful.

Then the sun comes up,
the birds singing,
news programs welcoming the morning.
Your body OK,
vegetables in the refrigerator,
sixteen inches unrealistic,
the night so distant,
desperation, loneliness,
darkness forgotten...

until two o'clock the next morning
when you rejoin the vibrant loud
artificial promises of perfection
on your couch
while the world sleeps,
fantasizing about beauty
and cleanliness, vitamins, inches,
$19.95, four payments.

It just seems so easy!
It almost seems real.

THE DINER

It is Halloween
at 3am and we are at the diner.

Me, at the bar,
Michael Meyers at the table in the corner.

Some bloody women
at the table by the door.

A Ninja Turtle
downing his seventh cup of coffee.

Three women in sex-costumes
laughing at their boyfriends' cowboy hats.

Me, unable to sleep, after nightmares
even a Halloween costume couldn't capture

eating tasteless eggs,
my fifth refill of Diet Pepsi.

The waiter at the bar
remembers I told him I was single,

reminds me he invited me
to his wrestling match.

The drunk man to my right
asks me what my costume is.

I tell him it's a work uniform.
I'm not lying, I couldn't sleep

so I walked here at 3am.
The taxis thought I was lost,

honked at me,
but the diner is around the corner.

They aren't supposed to refill the Pepsi
but I promised the waiter I'd go watch him one day.

The droop in my eyes is a permanent thing.
The bed is the enemy.

My mania is a costume
I wish I could take off.

I walk to work,
greet the first customer.

One hour in I fall asleep
on the register.

The manager doesn't
even ask how hard I partied last night.

Just wakes me up like he does
every other day of the week.

VALENTINE'S DAY

I wonder if the piercer
at the local tattoo shop
woke up Valentine's Day morning
knowing a woman
would walk in looking for a thrill.

On Valentine's Day,
I found myself
exhibiting my anatomy,
spread-eagle in a tattoo shop,
as you, the first man in two years
touched my body.

Was my empty visible?
My loneliness?

Did I reveal myself in my tremble,
my fear of useless unimportance
echoing through my system.

My useless was so thick in me,
all I ever noticed
was women and their body parts
ripe and ready,
floating down the street,
desired by passing men
even when the attention was not wanted;

their ungrateful sex
never knowing vacancy
quite like I did.

On your table
open and outstretched
you dressed me with iodine,
the burning not painful,
just intense rejuvenation of skin,

your latex gloves
like the condoms I never needed to buy,
your gloved finger tips
the closest thing to human
my nerve endings had felt in years.

When you finished,
after climax of needle
and blue jewel insertion,
re-clothed and smiling,

did you send me off
as just another rebel
experimenting with her wild side,

or did you see the hot-blooded minx,
with no one to share a pulse,
finding validation in touch on Valentine's Day.

After fifteen minutes,
eighty-five dollars,
ready to walk home
as a woman again.

VACANCY

The day I got into the white van
in the parking lot of the mental hospital
with the man I sometimes
saw in the store,
I climbed into the passenger seat,
he took me to the train station.

Two miles,
tinted windows, an empty
windowless back.

He did what he said,
I didn't have shell out for a taxi,
got to my train in time,
sat on the blue seat still intact.

Often, I did this:
get into cars with men.
Walk around the neighborhood
half-naked all night,
hoping for a bite.

Loneliness is a peculiar feeling.
Giving every inch of myself to the world,
waiting to be caught in a snare;
hoping someone would touch
anything at all.

Safely get where I'm going,

return to my empty room,
knowing even the worst
felt they could do better.

BLUES CLUES

I got this neat backpack on Amazon.
Has an illustration of a cartoon backpack
drawn on the back.
Reminds me of *Blues Clues*
if you really remember the show.

The other day some friends and I
were walking down the street
in one of those neighborhoods
where even the lampposts smoke crack,
the kind where it's easy to make friends
if you've got a dollar,

and this guy, how old was he,
twenty-five? twenty-six?
a cracked mirror,
came over to stare at my bag.
I really stick out with that thing.

I love your backpack!
It's the dog, it's the dog!
What the hell was its name?

I yelled *Blues Clues!*
down the pavement to
a smile we could share.

A yelling, dancing
weave through litter and smoke.
Moonlit cereal,
school buses,
lunch lines,
living room,

home,
childhood,
human.

BARS

I keep working till midnight,
hitting the bars.
I'm twenty-two and they are all my age;
first time I've been
out in the wild and have access.

They're all smoking cigarettes
at the outdoor tables
with hamburgers at midnight
and their beer.

I am one of you! I think loudly
so that they hear me, in my skirts
that fit nice, breaking free
from the group home finally.

I am one of you! We are the same age!
Can you tell I broke the chains!
Can you tell my sedatives haven't kicked in!
Can you tell I'm here and ready for sex
love, a social life, a mainstream boyfriend!

I am invisible in the shadow,
anyway I don't know what to say
to them so I hide by the bouncer,

big man like the staff
who made sure the door was locked
at night. Sway with the music.

Ten minutes after I arrive
my medicine kicks in.
I slowly walk home, proud:
They've seen me at last

MY LIBIDO, MY CHOICES

I am committed after a breakup.
After watching him come into my job
with his next girlfriend,
wave at me as he
puts his arm around her,
they walk through the beer aisle.

The wind tunnel in my gut
propelling me into the psyche ward.
A vacation to get away from
this heartbreak of a neighborhood.

Nina I've slept with two girls
since we broke up. You've been crying,
dyeing your hair, piercing your nipples
no one has taken you out yet.

The man sits at the table in a nightgown
with a sock on missing toes,
thirty-eight years old to my to my twenty-four.
We play UNO, eat lunch together.

Twelve hours before I get discharged
I realize finally someone wants some of this.

So we kiss.
Derek with his rap sheet,
missing toes,
prison sentence,
no home to leave to,
no money,
just two soft lips.

My ex and Derek
calling my number now.
My ex to ask how I met a convict.
Did Honey Bear go to the precinct?
Is she really this lonely?
Derek still committed,
Nina do you remember that kiss?

CHURCH STEPS

The woman who lives on the church steps
waves *hi* to us every morning
as we walk to kindergarten
so we always wave back.

Wild red curly hair,
pink cheeks,
red blanket
draped across a bit of cardboard.

Our school costs
as much as college
if you see the bill,

but we wave.

In ninth grade on vacations
I pack bags for the homeless
with stale bagels and boxed juice,
hang out with them during lunch.

The summer before junior year
I work at the local food pantry.

I barely graduate.

Five years later
I'm living in a group home.
It's time for Christmas donations.
Someone leaves a winter coat,

it fits.

Five years later
I'm living one step up from a homeless shelter.
I run out of money so I raid the pantry.
Mealworms turn to moths.
Then. Bedbugs. Everywhere.
Because half of us are from
jail or the shelter.

At Thanksgiving
volunteers serve us donated turkey.

The redhead on the
church steps dies of exposure.

The kids from the high school
across the street wave *hello.*

I smile,
wave back.

CREDIT CARDS AND CELL PHONES

Hello, thank you for picking up.
After all those choices I was beginning to lose hope.
It's lonely here, in my bedroom.
Your voice feels so close
even though you're continents away.

No, I don't need to pay my bill,
my service is fine.
I don't need overdraft protection,
don't want a new credit card.
I only wanted to hear someone else's voice besides mine
ricocheting through this empty room.

Why is the only personal question you are allowed to ask
How are you this evening?
Do you have so many other calls pulsing through the switchboard?
Do they monitor us at one o'clock in the morning,
chatting, having satisfied that your services are otherwise unneeded?
Do you have to alter your accent to match mine?
What is the weather like outside your cubicle?
Do you even work in a cubicle?
What does your hair look like, mine is disheveled.
I couldn't sleep again.
I was up thinking thoughts that were too loud,
decided to call you.

No, I guess there's nothing else you can help me with.
Yes, I will give you a good report.
No, you don't have to worry,
you solved my problem perfectly.

HOTEL

A hotel.
Piece of art.
Tenants and their luxuries.
Starbucks in the lobby.
Coffee for ten bucks.
Ceiling murals.
Free water bottles.
Thirty-dollar breakfast.

Outside a man on the corner.
His cat quiet on a milk crate.
Empty cup for change.

Night falls.
Everyone turning
down their sheets.

A man snuggles with his cat.
Curls up in the shadow
of the building.
Falls asleep.

THE STAR OF THE SHOW

Everybody Loves Raymond
was not about the twins,
the blonde daughter
playing in the background.

Canned laughter, adult jokes.
She complains about him,
he complains about her,

there's a child somewhere
drinking apple juice.
No one cares.

One of the twins
committed suicide this year.
The tabloids and the news announcing:
Child star's tragic death.
Flashing a picture of him at seven,
he was a young adult now.

When people commit suicide
we are all their friends.
There are eulogies
from the bullies,
cheerleaders.

Background child star
denied even canned laughter.

Finally, the star of the show.

PART TWO:

The Saving of Things

WIZARD

There is a girl with a
bottle of sleeping pills
at the register.

Sweater stenched with mildew,
ratty hair, sneakers ripped apart
from toenails unclipped.

There with a credit card, tremor.

The phone rings, her father.
The pills get placed on the counter.

Nina! I saw you called!
I remembered this great quote.
Are you by Barnes and Noble?
Go and buy "A Once and Future King".
Find the Merlin quote,
The best thing for being sad
is to learn something.
It's there at the end
of one of the chapters.

There is a bottle of pills
in the return bin.
A girl sprinting to a bookstore
before it closes.

MERRY CHRISTMAS

In NYC the neighborhoods are never empty,
but on Christmas they're mostly empty,
the stores all closed,

so my sister and I wander the streets;
two Jewish girls walking the grey,
snow covered sidewalks
matching the sky.

The newspaper stand
has the gate open.
I'm thirsty like always.

Nice Muslim man takes the dollar.
Merry Christmas! We celebrate,
into the echo of the empty corner.

Merry Christmas! He calls after us,
you can almost hear the bells jingling
on my can.

Three strangers to Christmas
still festive,
welcoming the season,
out on a cold winter day.

MALL WALKERS

In the early morning,
before the crowds rack up their parents'
credit cards on clothes and greasy food court stains,
before the Muzak is turned on,
escalators not yet begun their conveyor-belt journey,
the elderly own the mall.
In sweatpants and tee-shirts
they walk past dark storefronts,
inactive fountains,
up the still escalators,
around and around for hours.

In pairs sometimes or alone,
panting and moving
in the still air before the first employees
have even left their houses to come to work.

This phenomenon in every mall;
doors never locked, lights left on,
carpeted laps are trodden on repeat.

When I wake up too early to find company
I walk to the mall.
Enter a morning universe of people
who don't acknowledge my bloodshot eyes,
care what I am doing there,
passing smiles and sighs
at how we all become out of breath
after climbing from floor to floor.

THROUGH THE GAP

New Yorkers have reputations
for not caring too much.

Any foreigner watching the news
will tell you we walk alone, strangers,

avoiding friendly communication,
community, common decency.

Stabbings on every street corner,
convenience store holdups,
we are solid, can't be cracked.

I was on my way to recite poetry.
Metro-North train delivers poet to Grand Central,
Grand Central delivers poet to subway,
subway train stops at Union Square,

with the biggest gap in the subway system.

Here is where I daydream,
here is where hurried subway riders
jostle and push me,
until I fall halfway down the gap
between the train and the platform.

I don't know who saw me first.
Strong hands beneath shaking shoulders fling

daydreaming girl from one minute to lost legs
to standing upright.

A fading question, *are you OK?*
I turn to answer, no one is waiting for my response.

Accident prone stranger saved
by New York City angels,
abandoning the platform
before she sees who saved her.

Hardened New Yorkers
knowing the rarity of thank you.

Seconds later, only a memory,
the bell announcing the doors are closing,

The automated voice warning, *Please, mind the gap.*

(For the angels at the Union Square 6 train station)

PANCAKES AND ORANGE JUICE

A man and a woman walk into a diner
the waiter brings them water
they order breakfast.

A man and a woman walk into a diner
have nothing to say.

A man and a woman walk into a diner
smell like last night.

A man and a woman walk into a diner
smile over the second round
of drinks they've shared.

A man and a woman walk into a diner
wonder how long they have to talk
before the date is over.

A man and a woman went on a twelve-hour date
starting last night and this is how they finish it.

A man and a woman walk into a diner,
at least they still shared breakfast.

I wonder if he held her all night,
if there will be another.

Wonder if one day, with grandchildren on their knees
they'll remember how terrible the coffee is here,

how drunk they were, had nothing to talk about.
How neither of them knew this was the beginning.

BOW

When he was leaving I cried.
During the English class
I was taking to forget him,
the bus ride home,
into the groceries I sold,
on the sidewalk,
in the laundry room.

I cried on the train,
in the taxis,
at 6am on the way to work.

If there was a flood
it was because
I filled the streets.
If the levees overflowed,
it was because of me.

And one by one,
my classmates,
people on the bus,
in the grocery store,
overnight taxi driver,
took my hand
and said they'd pray.

The woman chanting
Jesus help this girl
in 7/11,
the gentleman
paying with food stamps,
the kid sitting next to me in class.

All together, for months, until he left.

And though I didn't believe them,
wanted something more practical,
I didn't tell them that.
I bent my head down,
closed my eyes,
let them take my hand.

LEARNING TO SAY NO

staff bed checks were always the closest thing to a boyfriend
it's been eight years since you left
the dreams are still vivid
you've been so lonely
sending the email so easy
you didn't expect him to respond
if you ask about his wife then it's not really a date
just coffee
he's forty now
you're twenty-eight
still the same time of night as it used to be
you weren't even sure if the email would work
just you were lonely
if you ask about his wife it's just coffee
he still remembers all the important things
you still remember all the important things
sometimes the closest thing to a boyfriend
is those mandatory bed checks
testosterone by the light switch
closest escape from lonely
he is always online
you haven't been sleeping
if you mention his wife it's just talking
when he hugs you goodnight you feel the ache of a decade
if it's every saturday night it might be dating
you're not sure
he just responds
a guaranteed yes
no boundary of title
the fantasy
spitting out of the pages of your poems
he asks to crash on your sofa
you giggle
he says no man knows you like he does

you giggle
he says no woman should stay lonely forever
you tell him he's just a mentor
he drops you off
hugs you goodnight
you message him during insomnia
he always answered before
now
nothing.

TIMID MAN

Give me a timid man,
quiet and hidden.
Shy clammy hands sweaty at the thought of me,
wondering what my soft feels like,
whose fingers don't already know
the workings of my joints before we touch.

I want to be a soft note longed for like no other,
special body of keys,
newly learned chopsticks,
not routine practice.

I want a man who's not loved many women,
but loved the ones he has so hard.
Wants to kiss their lips but rarely does,
does not know how to sweet talk
shirt buttons open.

I want a wallflower who longs for dance partners,
sees the easy steps,
resting hand on the hip,
whispers in the ear, the dip,
imagines it is his fingers on the dress,
how he would remember the moment all weekend.

I don't have time for
the ones who know all the words already;
the dapper gentleman who predicts my yes
before I say it,
takes it like he's taken so many,
words practiced, rehearsed,
as though I'm just another piano
he can close down and walk away from
like he has so many times before.

No, I long for a heart startled
at my lips' graze,
my new and foreign stroke,
the pink dash on cheeks,
that first touch above the waist.

I long for arms familiar with empty,
the ones who feared they'd never fill.

The delicate kiss,
fallen knee,
that first sweet release
against my frame.

EPILOGUE

HOW TO LOVE SOMEONE WHO HAS NEVER BEEN LOVED (OR HOW TO LEARN TO LOVE AGAIN)

1.
The first time you touch him he will flinch.
He is an abandoned warehouse
which has not felt electricity
pump through its walls since it was built.
Your fingertips are the first lanterns to light the rooms,
his cold floors and windows were not anticipating their warmth.

The first time you kiss him he will turn away;
deny the touch he has long since deemed impossible.
Try again, be gentle.
Hold his hand in yours and squeeze until he softens.
Once his body realizes you are safe he will
unravel into your arms.

The first time he is in your bed
he will be unable to focus.
Move slowly and do not rush.
Keep his attention and show his body
that your touch is trustworthy,
that his skin has no reason to be afraid.

2.
The first time he touches your scars
do not tremble;
remember the desire is mutual this time,
that neither one of you is an unwilling party.
The dents left in your skin have had time to heal,
you are letting yourself relax
because he does not need to
be the one to sew you back together.

The first time you undress for him make eye contact.
Do not let your hesitation show.
His touch is not tainted this time, unhealthy,
your skin deserves his fingerprints.

The first time you make love,
you close your eyes anticipating the usual
discomfort and flashbacks you are accustomed to.
You prepare for your disassociation,
but his breath and kiss and hands do not feel uninvited.
You can open your eyes
without cringing for the first time.

3
When you realize that this is your first real intimacy
just as much as it is his,
hold him closer than you had planned.
Let him hold you as much
as his warehouse walls need to,
melt into his arms.

Light your fingertip lanterns,
fill him so that neither one of you
feels empty and barren again.
Smile and relax,

you are home now.

ACKNOWLEDGMENTS

I would like to acknowledge Wil Wynn, Adam Biggs, Nicole Homer, Mark Wedemeyer, Lucy Robins and Susan Leicher for helping me take this manuscript which has been written and re-written over and over and reshaped and re-formed so many times for over two years until becoming this poem book you have just finished.

Thank you for encouraging me
to make this poem book
the best it can be.

❖

"Boy in the Bathroom" first appeared in
the anthology, *Condoms and Hot Tubs Don't Mix*
an Anthology of Awkward Sexcapades

"Church Steps" and "How to Love Someone"
first appeared in *Anti-Heroin Chic*

"Smolder" first appeared in *FreezeRay Poetry*

"Valentine's Day" first appeared
in *VanillaSex* Magazine

"The Diner" first appeared in *Waymark* Magazine

"Vacancy" and "Quiet Car" first appeared
in *Raw Art Review*

PRAISE FOR *T. GONDII*

Having had the pleasure of reading all three of this author's published books, it is no surprise that she continues to amaze and move me with her poetry. Her collection takes you on a journey, and draws you into her world, full of pain and love, and of course cats! She is an inspiration to me, and I cannot recommend this (and her other two books) highly enough!
—*Deb Klein*

❖

I loved reading this. I especially appreciated "To my Future Mother in Law" and "Consent." Not only is this well written, it makes me feel less alone. I love the raw honesty and total exposure on these pages. Nina perfectly captures so many of the things I've experienced. Reading this felt like sitting down with a friend who gets it. —*KH*

❖

"Buy the ticket, take the ride" This is an amazing collection of thoughts, struggles and stories of a truly amazing woman. This collection does not disappoint. —*Thanh Wisler*

BY THE AUTHOR OF "SUPERMARKET DIARIES" and "A BED WITH MY NAME ON IT"

t. gondii

Nina Belén Robins

T. GONDII
Nina Belén Robins

With searing honesty and ferocious wit, noted poet and mental health advocate Robins illuminates the brutal internal and external pressure to bear children; and the courage, self-awareness, love — and pain — required to remain child-free. Just when her words become near-unbearable, she throws in a sly and hilarious poem about cats.

PRAISE FOR *A BED WITH MY NAME ON IT*

Bookended by movingly hopeful poems, this collection carries the reader into places we may never have been and may hope never to go to. But having been there and come through—with the writer—with humor, deep humanity, and an energizing self-acceptance, we're better for it. These poems have the music of performance poetry in them and the power of crafted literary work. We have here a very satisfying and rare merger of talent, humility and valuable life experience. No poem fell flat for me. Every poem invites and rewards multiple readings.—*Elizabeth K. Gordon*

❖

If you have ever had a moment that made you feel out of control, this book has a poem for you. Several, in fact, and not one of them gives you a feeling of anything less than survival at its finest.Don't forget this poet's name. Nina will have a long career. You won't forget the poetry.— *Wil Gibson*

❖

I read this book in one sitting! Nina brought us into her life and spread light into so many places so often left in the dark. It was a pleasure to share her perspective. I work with girls in a community residence and I could relate to each page with the girls I have worked with as well as my own personal experiences. This was so powerful.—*Amanda*

❖

Nina's book *A Bed with my Name on It* is tragic beauty. The poems are filled with so much raw emotion, each one is like a gut punch of "damn." I'm very grateful for her poems.—*Nick Yuk*

A BED
WITH MY
NAME
ON IT

Nina Belén Robins

This book of poems draws on the
author's experience within the
mental health system from the
time she was a little girl until she
reached her early twenties. The
poems illuminate the soul-numb-
ing degradations that spurred her
to find her way out of the system
and the kindnesses that made it
possible.

PRAISE FOR *SUPERMARKET DIARIES*

This magnificent volume of poetry is the author's first published book but surely not her last. With impeccable insight and a vivacious appreciation for the human condition, Robins takes us on a journey behind the supermarket check-out counter. She offers us a unique glimpse into the lives of the ordinary people who cross her path each day, using her incredible poetic talents to convince us of the extra-ordinary humanity of each of them, and by extension, of ourselves. I highly recommend this book! — *choirqueer*

❖

Simple observations, expressed with great insight, wisdom and eloquence. — *Dan Couture*

❖

In a variety of stories through the eyes of a creatively observant cashier, Nina's writing is sharp witted, emotional, and promises to be very memorable! — *Zadra*

❖

This is *The Spoon River Anthology* of supermarkets: insightful poems about customers, staff and life behind the cash register, by an exciting young NYC poet. Can't wait for the next book! — *Lori Ubell*

SUPER-
MARKET
DIARIES

Nina Belén Robins

Mild-mannered grocery store employee by day, Nina Robins is a well-known performance poet who has twice performed at the National Poetry Slam. Her poetry has been described as "exceptionally appealing," "heartbreakingly honest," and "subversively deep for work so overtly entertaining."

—Taylor Mali, author of
What Teachers Make